DATE DUE

JUL 05 1996	MAY 2 2 2000	
JUL 2 3 1996	JAN 1 9 2001	
AUG 07 1996	APR 3 0 2001	
AUG 1 9 1996	JUN 2 5 2001	
SEP 1 7 1996	MAY 2 4 2003	
OCT 08 1996	JUL 0 1 2003	
MAR 1 5 1997		
MAR 3 1 1997		
MAY 2 1 1997		
OCT 2 2 1997		
NOV 2 4 1997		
MAR 0 9 1998		
APR 2 5 1998		
SEP 2 8 1998		
OCT 2 1 1998		
JAN 1 9 1999		
NOV 2 3 1999		
APR 1 3 2000		

GAYLORD   PRINTED IN U.S.A

Wonders of the Rain Forest

Written by Janet Craig

Illustrated by S.D. Schindler

Troll Associates

Metric Equivalents

1 foot   = 30.5 centimeters

1 pound = .45 kilogram

1 acre   = .40 hectare

Library of Congress Cataloging-in-Publication Data

——

    Wonders of the rain forest.

    Summary: Discusses the animals and plants which
give such color and beauty to tropical rain forests
and jungles.
    1. Rain forest ecology—Juvenile literature.
[1. Rain forests.   2. Jungles]   I. Schindler, S.D.,
ill. II. Title.
QH541.5.R27P35   1990   574.5'2642   89-5001
ISBN 0-8167-1763-X (lib. bdg.)
ISBN 0-8167-1764-8 (pbk.)

Copyright © 1990 by Troll Associates

Printed in the United States of America, bound in Mexico.

10 9 8 7 6 5

It is dawn in the rain forest. On this hot sunny morning, steam rises from the trees. Far away, a rushing waterfall can be heard. What mysteries does the warm, wet forest hold? Whose home is it?

At first, the forest seems like a still, almost empty place. Seen from above, the treetops look like a giant umbrella. It is an umbrella made from patches of every shade of green. Tall trees grow so closely together that the ground below cannot be seen. Every so often a tree taller than the rest spreads its wide branches.

Look carefully among the trees. There are many surprises to be found. Here and there, a giant white or red flower adds a spot of color. A flock of brightly colored birds suddenly takes flight. And here is a monkey. At first it is still and nearly invisible among the branches. Then, with a loud chatter, off the monkey goes, swinging through the trees.

Rain forests, known for their warm weather and almost daily rain showers, are the home of millions of plants and animals. Rain forests cover only one-twelfth of the earth, but they are filled with life. In fact, about half of all kinds of plants and animals in the world are found there.

Rain forests grow in tropical parts of the world, in South and Central America, in Africa and Asia, and in the islands of the Pacific Ocean.

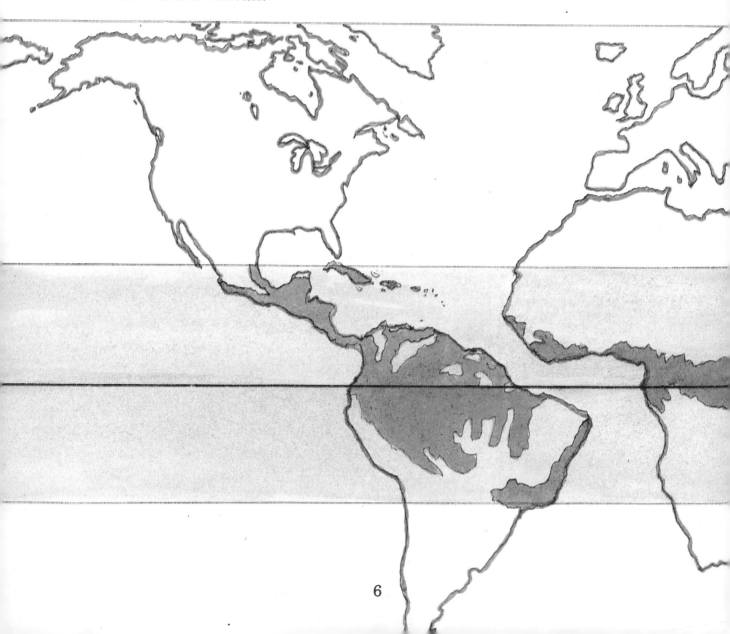

Tropical lands lie near the equator, the imaginary line that circles the earth. Near the equator, the seasons do not change very much. The weather is hot all year round. This makes it easy for many kinds of plants and animals to live and grow in the rain forest.

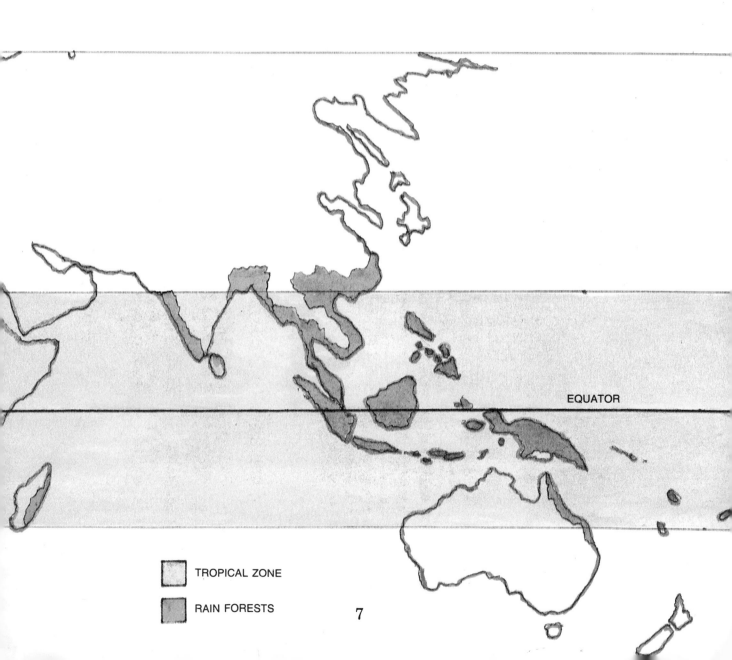

EQUATOR

☐ TROPICAL ZONE

▨ RAIN FORESTS

7

In cooler parts of the world, the weather and seasons change. It gets warmer in the summer and colder in the winter. Plants grow mostly in the warmer months and many lose their leaves in the cooler months. Plants and trees that lose their leaves are called deciduous.

Most trees in the tropical rain forest stay green year round. As old leaves die and fall to the ground, new leaves are always ready to take their place.

In cooler parts of the world, groups of the same type of tree often grow together. One part of the forest may have mostly pine trees; another part may be filled with oaks. In rain forests, though, more than a hundred different kinds of trees can grow together in one small area. Scientists have recently found a place in South America where there are over three hundred different kinds of trees growing on two and a half acres (1 hectare) of land!

No section of the huge rain forest is quite like any other part. And of all the rain forests in the world, no two are exactly alike. A unique, or special group of animals and plants lives in each forest.

Plants grow quickly in the rain forest. In Asia, some kinds of bamboo grow more than a foot a day. And certain plants that we know as small plants grow to a giant size in the rain forest. One example is the tiny violet of North America. It can grow to be 30 feet (9 m) tall in the South American rain forest.

Scientists who study the rain forest divide it into layers. Each layer forms an *ecosystem*, a special place where certain plants and animals can live together.

The top layer of the forest is called the *upper canopy*. It is made of the tallest trees, which grow to 120 feet (36.5 m) high or higher. The trees reach above all else, stretching for the precious sunlight they need.

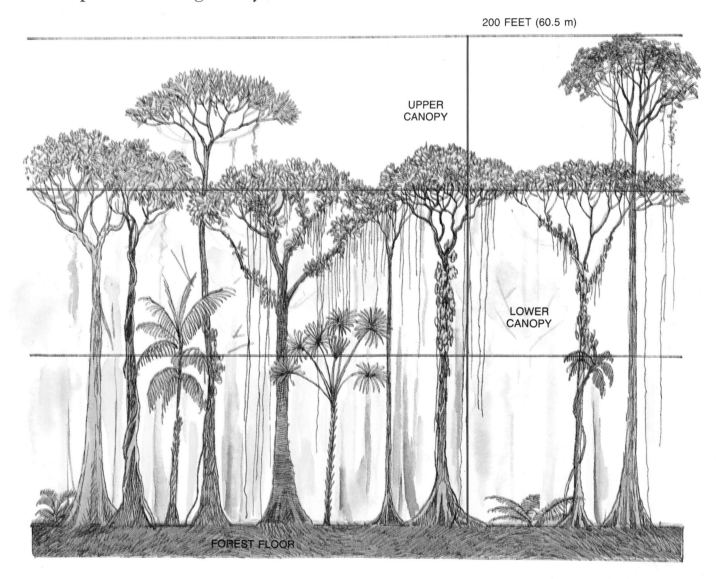

200 FEET (60.5 m)

UPPER CANOPY

LOWER CANOPY

FOREST FLOOR

Below the upper canopy is the *lower canopy* of plants and trees. It begins at about 30 feet (9 m) above the ground and reaches 90 feet (27 m).

Heavy vines, called lianas, hang among the branches. Looping and knotting about the trees, the lianas twist into an endless tangle.

Air plants grow on the branches of many trees. These special plants do not have roots. They get all their food and water from the air. Many orchids, mosses, and ferns are air plants. By perching upon the tree branches, air plants are able to get closer to the sunlight.

Scientists think two-thirds of all the plants and animals of the forest live in the upper and lower canopies. Some animals are born in the treetops and spend their whole lives there. They never once set foot upon the ground.

The ground is the lowest layer of the forest. It is called the *forest floor*. Here it is very dark and wet. Little or no sunlight reaches the forest floor where ferns, mosses, and fungi grow.

Although the upper canopy of the forest is thick and tangled with plants, the floor is nearly empty. Without sunlight, far fewer plants can live there. So it is easy to find a path among the wide tree trunks.

Strong supports, called buttress roots, surround some of the largest tree trunks. These wide roots help to hold up the heavy weight of the tree.

Here and there grows another type of tree called the strangler fig. This plant begins as an air plant on the branch of another tree. Slowly, the fig sends down long, thin roots. These roots twine about the other tree, slowly strangling it. At last, the strangler fig stands tall. Its roots are strong, and its branches have reached the light. The fig tree has won the battle—and the tree that it grew upon soon dies.

You might think that because of the many plants that grow in the rain forest, the soil must be very rich. But this is not so. The top soil of the rain forest is thin because rain is always washing it away. It is mainly the warmth and wetness of the weather that helps the plants grow.

The mixtures of plants and animals that live in each layer of the forest are fascinating.

In the upper canopy of the South American forest, it's a sunny morning. The butterflies are out. They gather nectar from the hundreds of orchids and other flowers that dot the treetops.

Some of the butterflies blend in perfectly with the plants— that is their protection from birds and other animals that might like to eat them. Others, like the bright yellow *funeral moth*, are easily seen. But birds do not often eat this kind of moth. Any bird that does becomes sick from the poison in the moth's body.

The many fruits and flowers of the upper canopy offer plenty to eat for hummingbirds, bats, monkeys, and insects. In return, these animals do an important job for the plants. The animals take pollen and seeds from flowers and fruits and bring them to other parts of the forest. In this way, new plants are able to grow.

With thickly tangled branches and heavy wooden vines hanging from tree to tree, the upper canopy makes a wonderful home for an acrobat. Who are the forest acrobats? Many kinds of monkeys and apes are!

In the Asian forest, gibbons swing gracefully from branch to branch. These brownish apes search for insects, eggs, flowers, and fruit to eat.

A baby orangutan clings closely to its mother's side. Off they go for a treetop ride. The mother ape is quite at home among the trees. She uses a hand-over-hand movement to swing along. Her feet, which look very much like hands, help her to climb.

Birds of every color and size also live among the treetops. The fiercest and biggest is the harpy eagle of the Amazon forest in South America. From its nest in the highest tree, the harpy takes flight. Its spotted feathers help it blend in among the shadows. It glides along in search of a monkey or bird to eat.

In the lower canopy, hundreds of sleeping bats hang upside down from tree branches. The bats sleep by day and hunt for insects by night.

A vine hangs motionless from a branch. Suddenly, it moves! It is not a plant at all, but the vine snake of West Africa. Its color and the way it poses among the vines make this animal hard to spot. When a tasty meal of frog or lizard comes along, the "vine" springs into action.

Many kinds of insects live along the forest floor. One of the best known is the army ant. Marching through the forest in an army that is twenty million strong, these ants can eat a sick or wounded animal in only a few minutes. The ants march on, and all that is left behind are the animal's bones.

Exploring the rain forest offers a rich variety of sights and sounds. The sound of a river can be heard in the distance. Movement through the forest becomes more difficult near the river. The trees are not so tall, and the land is more open. Here the sunlight lets plants grow closer to the ground. Tangled shrubs, vines, and grasses make it almost impossible to find a path. This kind of dense, overgrown place is called a jungle.

In South America, the Amazon River cuts through the jungle. The *capybara* stops to drink at the edge of the river. This animal, which looks like a giant guinea pig, is the largest rodent in the world.

In the river stands a stork. It quickly flies away when it sees a crocodile swimming near.

One of the jungle's largest hunters is the 300-pound (135-kg) jaguar. This South American jungle cat has a yellowish and black-spotted coat. Its spots help this cat to hide among the shadows and spots of light in the jungle.

The jaguar likes to go fishing. It dips its tail in the water. When a curious fish swims near, the jaguar quickly pounces.

Jungles are often found near tropical river banks in the rain
forests of the world. People living in the jungle often make their
homes along river banks.

Although it is a difficult place to live, people have always made their homes in rain forests and jungles. Some are farmers who raise crops on small bits of land.

Sometimes farmers clear the land for planting by the slash and burn method. Trees are cut down and then burned. The farmer plants crops here for a few years. Then, when the soil is no longer rich enough, the farmer moves on to a new place.

Many kinds of people live in jungles. Tribes of Pygmies live
in Central Africa. The Pygmies are not farmers. They live by
hunting for food and gathering wild fruits and plants to eat.
For other things they need, the Pygmies trade with farmers.

Some people have tried to harvest and sell some of the natural riches of the rain forest. Rubber, bamboo, minerals, and timber are just a few of these valuable products.

Rain forests give off oxygen to the world—a most important resource for people. Many scientists fear that too much of the world's rain forests are being cut down or changed. When rain forests are destroyed, the animals and plants that live there can not always survive in new places. Some of them may die out and become extinct.

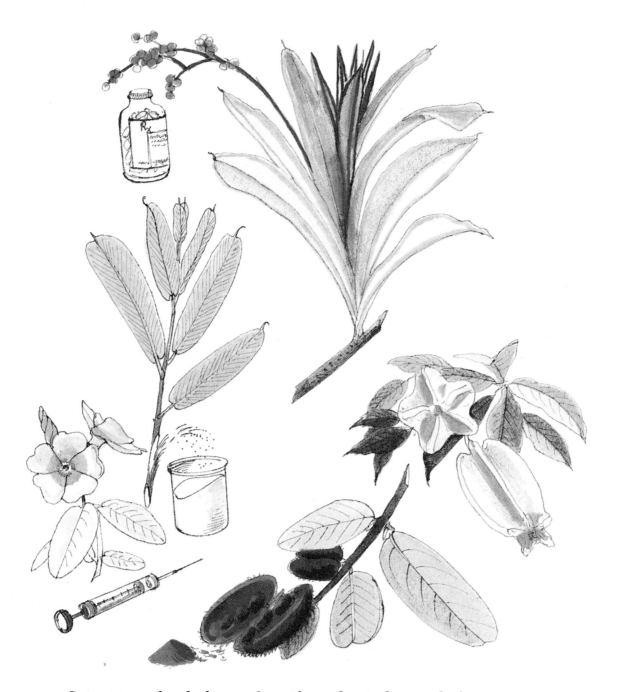

Scientists also believe that if used wisely, such forests can give us much-needed products. New medicines and new types of food could be developed from plants that grow in the rain forest.

It is difficult to study rain forests, but scientists wish to learn far more about them. In a way, rain forests are the last frontier on earth, for they still contain many mysteries we wish to solve. Rich with the treasures of life, rain forests and jungles can help us learn much about our planet.